VEHICLES Colour by Number

Cars, Trucks, Planes and more

Ages 4 - 8

M. Power

Introduction

Vehicles are machines used to carry and move people or things, for example *cars, buses, and airplanes.*

We at *M. Power Publications* have decided to compile beautiful coloring by number pages about all kinds of vehicles such as airplanes, rockets, trucks, trains, bicycles, and more coloring activities.

We hope you enjoy them very much.

 mpowerbooks  M. Power  powermbooks

This Book Belongs To:

_ _ _ _ _ _ _ _ _ _ _ _

_ _ _ _ _ _ _ _ _ _ _

1- Mustard   2- Red   3- Light green   4- White
5- Turquoise   6- Yellow   7- Gray   8- Black

1- Yellow   2- Blue   3- Brown   4- White
5- Light blue   6- Gray

9

1- Gray   2- Yellow   3- Turquoise   4- Black
5- Green   6- Light green

11

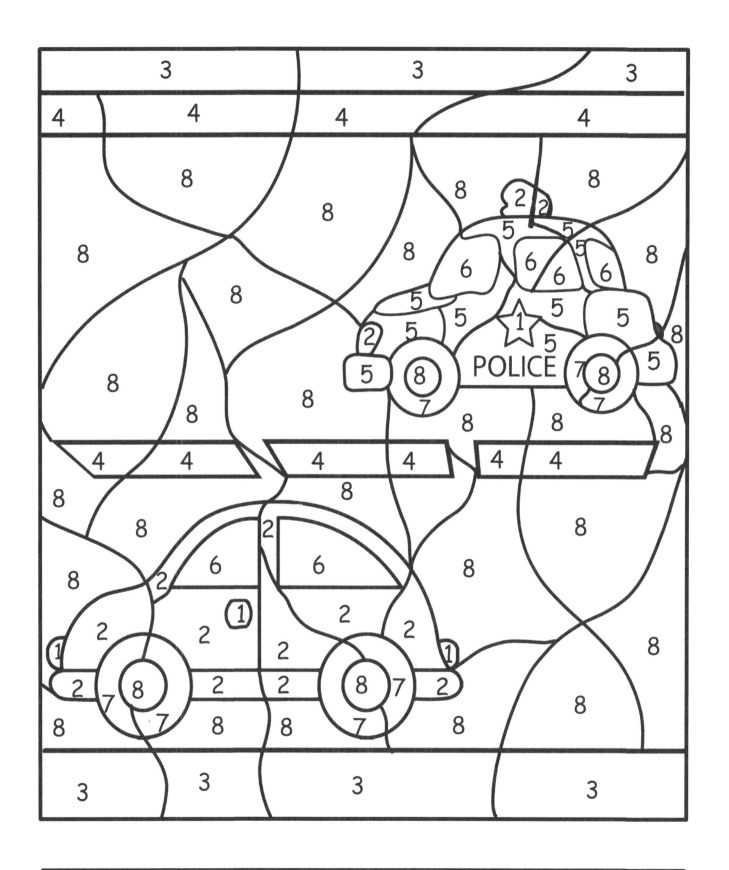

1- Yellow   2- Red   3- Green   4- White
5- Blue   6- Light blue   7- Black   8- Gray

13

1- Blue   2- Cream   3- Red   4- White
5- Gray   6- Yellow

1- Turquoise   2- Cream   3- Red   4- Yellow
5- White   6- Gray   7- Blue

1- Yellow   2- Cream   3- Red   4- Green
5- Brown   6- Black   7- Gray   8- Light green

19

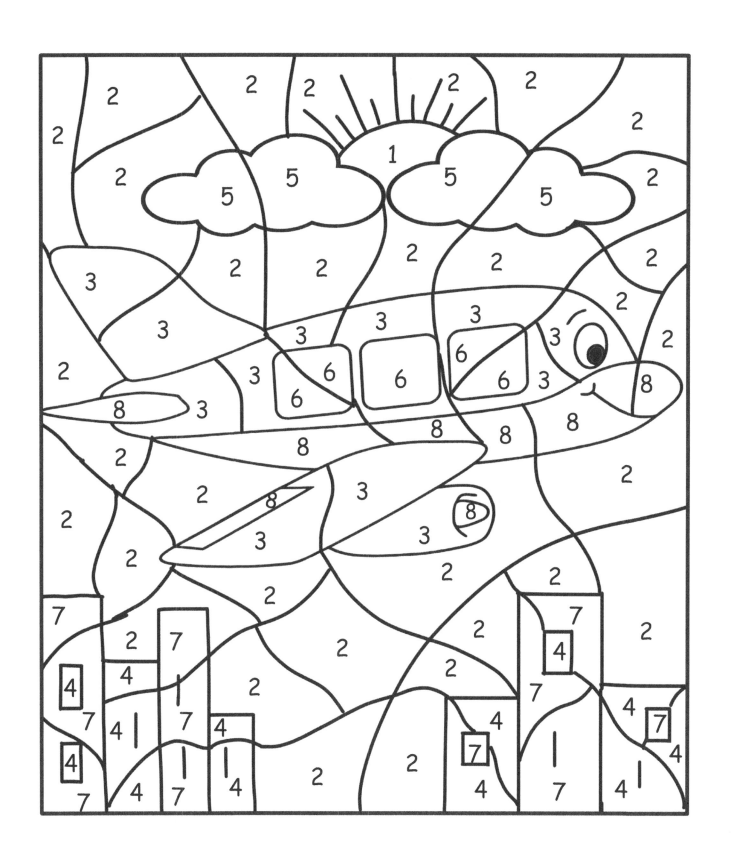

1- Yellow   2- Cream   3- Red   4- Green
5- White   6- Light blue   7- Purple   8- Gray

21

1- Orange   2- Cream   3- Purple   4- Green
5- Yellow   6- Turquoise   7- Gray

23

1- Red   2- Green   3- Light blue   4- Cream
5- Brown   6- Turquoise   7- Gray   8- Light green

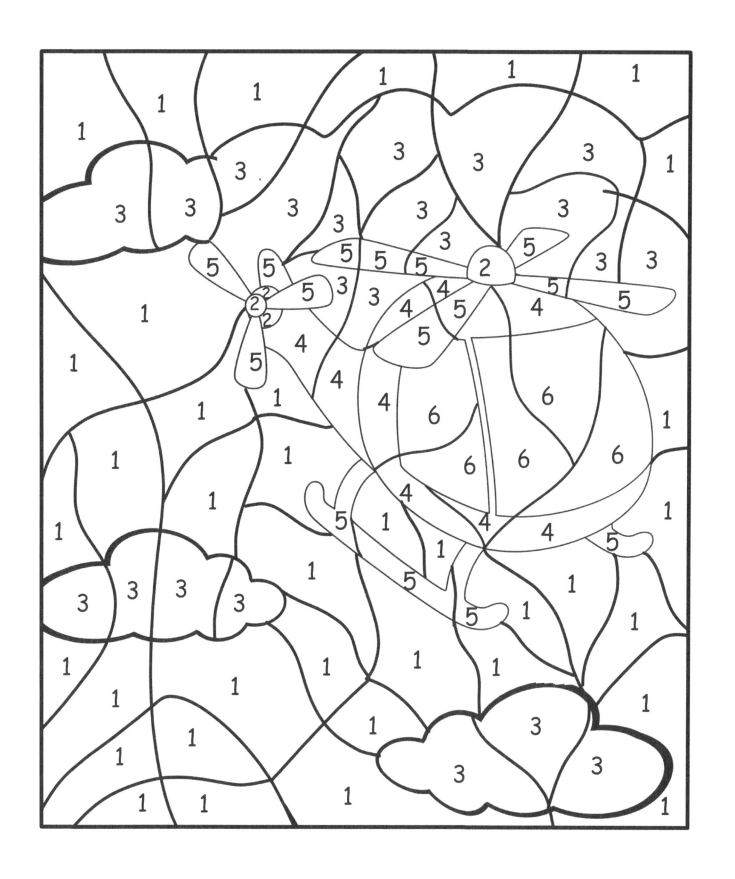

1- Blue   2- Mustard   3- White   4- Green
5- Gray   6- Orange

27

1- Brown   2- Cream   3- Red   4- Green
5- Mustard 6- Light blue   7- Gray   8- Turquoise

1- White   2- Red   3- Yellow   4- Gray
5- Blue   6- Black   7- Light blue

31

1- Mustard   2- Red   3- Light blue   4- Light green
5- Black   6- Gray

1- Brown   2- Cream   3- Light blue   4- White
5- Blue   6- Black   7- Yellow   8- Turquoise

1- Orange   2- Yellow   3- Red   4- Green
5- Purple   6- Blue   7- Light blue

1- Black   2- Red   3- Yellow   4- Orange
5- White   6- Cream   7- Gray   8- Blue

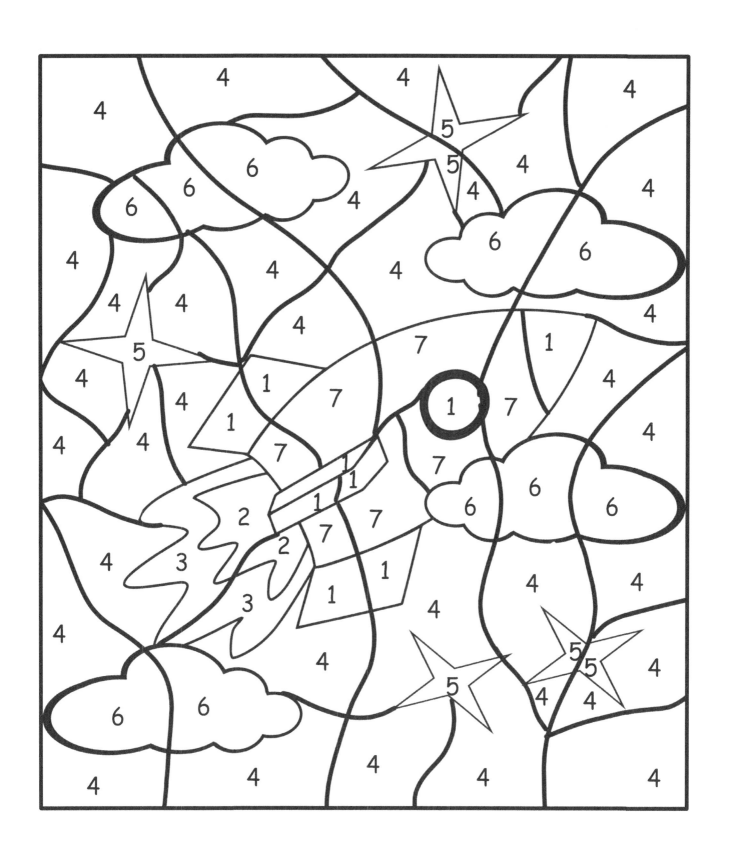

1- Green   2- Cream   3- Red   4- Blue
5- Yellow   6- White   7- Gray

1- Orange 2- Cream 3- Yellow 4- White
5- Blue 6- Light blue

1- Red   2- Light blue   3- Brown   4- Green
5- White   6- Gray   7- Black

45

1- Brown   2- Cream   3- Turquoise   4- Green
5- Black   6- Gray   7- Light green

1- Mustard   2- Purple   3- Light green   4- Green
5- Light blue   6- White

1- Mustard   2- Pink   3- White   4- Light green
5- Light blue   6- Turquoise   7- Gray

51

1- White   2- Yellow   3- Red   4- Green
5- Brown   6- Black   7- Gray   8- Light blue

1- Blue   2- Red   3- Black   4- Green
5- Light green   6- Gray

1- Gray   2- Cream   3- Orange   4- Green
5- Brown   6- Black   7- Yellow   8- Light blue

57

1- Mustard   2- Yellow   3- Turquoise   4- White
5- Light green   6- Blue   7- Gray

1- Mustard   2- Cream   3- White   4- Green
5- Light blue   6- Black   7- Gray   8- Light green

1- Yellow   2- White   3- Brown   4- Green
5-Turquoise   6- Gray   7- Light green

63

1- Brown   2- Orange   3- Gray   4- Green
5- Light blue   6- Light green   7- Black

1- Black   2- Cream   3- Purple   4- Green
5- Brown   6- Light green   7- Gray   8- Turquoise

1- Blue   2- White   3- Red   4- Yellow
5- Turquoise   6- Purple   7- Gray   8- Fuchsia

1- Gray   2- Yellow   3- Red   4- Green
5- Turquoise   6- Black   7- White   8- Light blue

71

1- Light green   2- Mustard   3- White   4- Green
5- Turquoise   6- Black   7- Gray   8- Light blue

1- Gray   2- Mustard   3- Blue   4- Green
5- White   6- Fuchsia   7- Red   8- Yellow

75

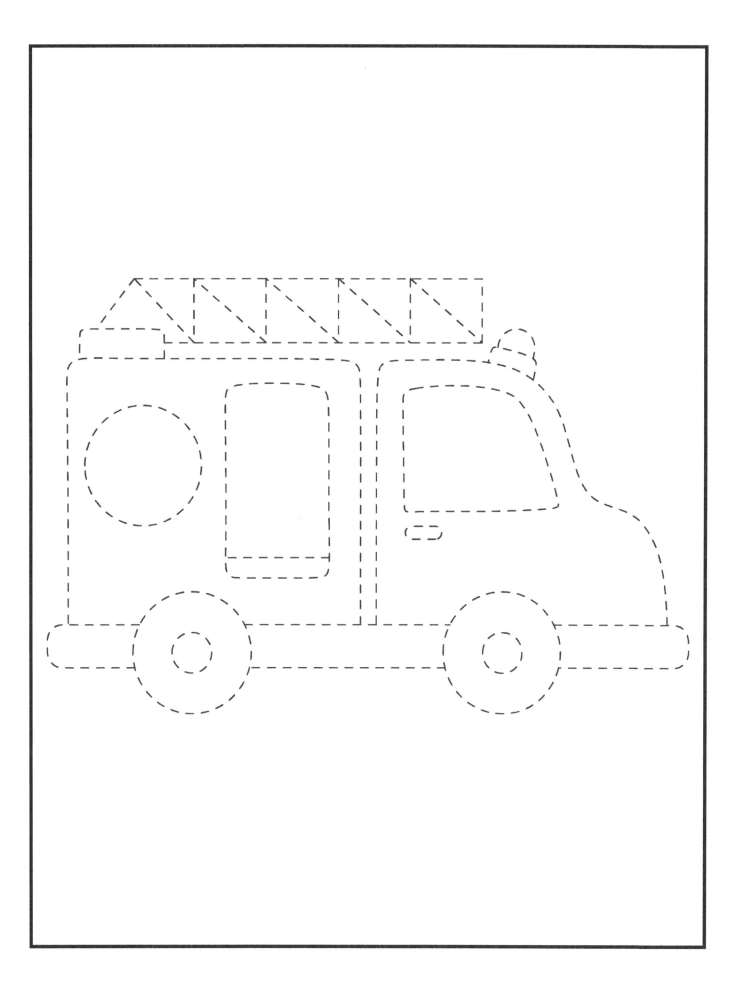

75

87

89

95

99

101

103

Made in the USA
Las Vegas, NV
04 November 2024

11069800R10059